Frantic Assembly
and the National Theatre of Scotland present

# BEAUTIFUL BURNOUT

by Bryony Lavery

D1374998

Beautiful Burnout was first performed on Saturday 7 August 2010
at Pleasance Forth, Edinburgh.

The Scottish
Government

Supported by
ARTS COUNCIL
ENGLAND

# Cast

*in alphabetical order*

| | |
|---|---|
| Ryan Fletcher | Cameron Burns |
| Eddie Kay | Steve George / Neil Neill |
| Vicki Manderson | Dina Massie |
| Lorraine M McIntosh | Carlotta |
| Taqi Nazeer | Ajay Chopra |
| Henry Pettigrew | Ainsley Binnie |
| Ewan Stewart | Bobby Burgess |

## Creative Team

| | |
|---|---|
| Bryony Lavery | Writer |
| Underworld | Music |
| Laura Hopkins | Designer |
| Andy Purves | Lighting Designer |
| Carolyn Downing | Sound Designer |
| Ian William Galloway | Video Designer |
| Anne Henderson | Casting Director |
| Simon Kenny | Assistant Designer |

Directed by Scott Graham and Steven Hoggett
Choreographed by the Directors with the Company

## Production Team

| | |
|---|---|
| Sunita Hinduja | Company Stage Manager |
| Nick Hill | Technical Stage Manager |
| Joni Carter | Stage Manager |
| Neill Pollard | Lighting Supervisor (rehearsals) |
| Andy Purves | Lighting Supervisor (tour) |
| Andrew Elliott | Sound Supervisor |
| Adam Young | Video Supervisor |
| Katy Lonsdale | Wardrobe Supervisor |
| Kat Smith | Wardrobe Technician |
| Hilary Cross | Wardrobe Technician |

# Thanks

**Frantic Assembly and the National Theatre of Scotland wish to thank the following individuals and organisations for their support.**

**Boxing Consultation and Training**
Kevin Smith, Terry McCormack (Lochend Amateur Boxing Club),
John McDermott (Blantyre Amateur Boxing Club), Peter MacKenzie
(Grip House, Glasgow), Cathal O'Grady (White Collar Boxing, Dublin),
Daniel Oyemomilara and John Rooney (Rooney's Gym, London).

**Boxing Research**
Brian Donald, Danny Lee (Greenock Amateur Boxing Club),
Donald Campbell, Dr Brian Tansey, Bruce Silverglade (Gleason's Gym,
Brooklyn).

**Development Workshops**
Ben Duke, Dan Wright, Emun Elliott, Geir Hytten, Jonathan Holt,
Keir Patrick, Laura McMonagle, Malcolm Shields, Paul Chaal and
Tony McGeever.

**Production**
The Jerwood Space, Fitness Takeaway in Airdrie, Guy Ramsay (Grip
House, Glasgow), Douglas Maxwell, Ros Steen (Voice and Dialect
Coach) Stuart McKirdy and Krista Vuori.

**Photography**
Ela Włodarczyk      Photograph of Taqi Nazeer (cover)
Johan Persson       Rehearsal shots

**Filming**
Trevor Henen        Director of Photography
Alex Taylor         Film Shoot Focus Puller
Michelle Lyons      Film Shoot Hair & Makeup
Tim Sandys          Tattoo artist

# Cast Biographies

## Ryan Fletcher

*Cameron Burns*

Ryan trained at the Royal Scottish Academy of Music and Drama.

Work for the National Theatre of Scotland includes *The Wolves in the Walls* (with Improbable), *365* (with Edinburgh International Festival), *Cockroach* and *Nobody Will Ever Forgive Us* (with Traverse, Edinburgh). Ryan also performed in the international and national tours of the multi-award winning *Black Watch*.

Ryan's other theatre credits include *The Costorphine Road Nativity* (Festival Theatre, Edinburgh), *The Last Witch* (Edinburgh International Festival/ Traverse, Edinburgh), *Confessions of a Justified Sinner* (Royal Lyceum, Edinburgh), *Turbo Folk, Cyrano de Bergerac, Water-proof, Ae Fond Kiss* and *Before I Go* (Òran Mór) .

Film and television credits include *Taggart, Scottish Killers, Filthy Rich, The Night Sweeper* and *Stop, Look, Listen*. Ryan was a series regular in *River City* for BBC Scotland.

## Eddie Kay

*Steve George / Neil Neill*

Eddie graduated in 1995 from the London Contemporary Dance School and Northern School of Contemporary Dance. He then taught and performed for four years in rural south-west England with Attic Dance Company.

Work for Frantic Assembly includes: *Hymns, Dirty Wonderland* and *Othello*. Other theatre work includes *Cost of Living, To Be Straight With You* (DV8 Physical Theatre) *Tranny Boy* (Legs on the Wall), *Knots, As You Are, Faun* (Coisceim Dance Company) and *Track* (Broken Talkers).

Work for the National Theatre of Scotland includes *Transform Caithness: Hunter* (as Associate Director) and *Transform Glasgow: Smiler* (as Movement Director).

Eddie is co-director of physical theatre company Big Man Wee Man and has choreographed and directed for Channel 4 (*Round 10*) and Freshmess (*Crash Test Human*).

## Vicki Manderson

*Dina Massie*

Vicki trained at the Scottish School of Contemporary Dance and London Contemporary Dance School.

Theatre and dance work includes *Invisible Dances* (International Dance Festival, Birmingham), *One Up One Down* (Gilmore Productions), *Dear Body* (Protein Dance), *Skylon Spirits* (Stan Won't Dance) and *Home Inverness* (National Theatre of Scotland).

Vicki is a Creative Learning Associate for Frantic Assembly. She has also been a member of Bare Bones Dance Company.

## Lorraine M McIntosh

*Carlotta*

Lorraine's first foray into professional acting was in 1998 in the Ken Loach award winning movie *My Name Is Joe*. Prior to this, she had concentrated solely on her career as a vocalist and musician with internationally successful band Deacon Blue. She is now also part of the duo McIntoshRoss with her husband Ricky, performing at the Glastonbury Festival 2010.

Theatre work includes *Sixteen* (Arches, Glasgow) and *Mum's the Word* (Robert C Kelly Productions).

Television work includes, *Hope Springs, Taggart, Psychos, Life Support* and three years as a regular cast member on BBC Scotland's *River City*.

Film work includes *Wilbur Wants to Kill Himself* and *Aberdeen*.

## Taqi Nazeer

*Ajay Chopra*

Taqi has recently graduated from the Royal Scottish Academy of Music and Drama, where he performed in plays such as *A Midsummer Night's Dream, Three Sisters* and *Black Snow*.

*Beautiful Burnout* is his professional acting debut.

## Henry Pettigrew

*Ainsley Binnie*

Henry trained at the Guildhall School of Music and Drama.

Theatre credits include *Troilus and Cressida* (Royal Shakespeare Company/ Edinburgh International Festival), *The Bevellers* (Citizens, Glasgow), *Black Watch* (National Theatre of Scotland) and *Hamlet* (Donmar West End /Broadway) for which he received an Ian Charleson Award commendation.

Television work includes *Midsomer Murders*, *The Relief of Belsen* and *Doctors*.

Radio work includes *The Sky at Midnight* and *The Family Man*.

## Ewan Stewart

*Bobby Burgess*

Ewan's recent theatre work includes *Dunsinane* (Royal Shakespeare Company), *Oh Go My Man, At the Table, Almost Nothing, Sacred Heart, Trade* and *Bluebird* (Royal Court, London), *Green Field* (Traverse, Edinburgh), and *The Duchess of Malfi* (Bristol Old Vic).

Television work includes *River City, Walter's War, Taggart, Rebus, Only Fools and Horses, Time of your Life, The Somme, Malice Aforethought, Dirty War* and *POW*.

Film work includes *Valhalla Rising, Eliminate Archie Cookson, One Last Chance, Conspiracy, Rob Roy, Titanic, Kafka, Stella Does Tricks, The Big Brass Ring* and *The Cook, The Thief, His Wife and Her Lover*.

# Creative Team Biographies

## Bryony Lavery

*Writer*

Bryony's plays include *Stockholm* (Wolff-Whiting Best Play 2008) for Frantic Assembly, *Last Easter* (Manhattan Classic Company), *A Wedding Story* (Sphinx) and *Frozen* (TMA Best Play 2001, Eileen Anderson Best Play 2001) which began life at Birmingham Rep, moved to the National Theatre, London, and was then produced on Broadway where it was nominated for four Tony awards. She has written five plays for National Theatre Connections.

Recent work includes *Kursk* (Sound and Fury), *The Wicked Lady* (New Vic, Stoke-on-Trent), *Stockholm* (Frantic Assembly/ Sydney Theatre Company) and, with Jason Carr, *A Christmas Carol* (Birmingham Rep/ West Yorkshire Playhouse).

Current projects include the opera *57 Hours in The House of Culture* with John Keane, Peter Wyer and Phyllida Lloyd, and *Lost and Found* (English Touring Theatre, London/ Brink Theatre, Adelaide).

Bryony is honorary Doctor of Arts at De Montford University and a Fellow of the Royal Society of Literature.

## Scott Graham

*Co-director/ Choreographer*

Scott is co-founder and Artistic Director of Frantic Assembly.

For Frantic Assembly, Scott has co-directed *Othello* (TMA award – Best Direction), *Stockholm, pool (no water), Dirty Wonderland, Rabbit, Peepshow* and *Underworld*. Director/performer credits include *Hymns, Tiny Dynamite, On Blindness, Heavenly, Sell Out, Zero, Flesh, Klub* and *Look Back in Anger*.

Scott's other directing credits include: *Home Inverness* (National Theatre of Scotland), *Kerching* (Sixth Sense), *It's A Long Road* (Polka Theatre) and *Up on the Roof* (Polka Theatre). Scott has also provided choreography and movement direction for *Cinderella* (Unicorn Theatre), *Frankenstein* (Royal and Dergnate), *The May Queen* (Liverpool Everyman), *Hothouse* and *Market Boy* (National Theatre, London), *Villette* (Stephen Joseph Theatre), *Vs* (Karim Tonsi Dance Company, Cairo), and *Improper* (Bare Bones Dance Company).

With Steven Hoggett and Bryony Lavery, Scott created *It Snows,* a National Theatre Connections play for 2008. With Steven Hoggett, Scott has written *The Frantic Assembly Book of Devising Theatre* (Routledge).

## Steven Hoggett

*Co-director/ Choreographer*

Steven is co-founder and Artistic Director of Frantic Assembly.

For Frantic Assembly, Steven has co-directed *Othello* (TMA award – Best Direction), *Stockholm, pool (no water), Dirty Wonderland, Rabbit, Peepshow* and *Underworld*.

Director/performer credits for the company include: *Hymns, Tiny Dynamite, On Blindness, Heavenly, Sell Out, Zero, Flesh, Klub* and *Look Back In Anger*.

As Associate Director (Movement), Steven worked on the multi award-winning production *Black Watch* (National Theatre of Scotland) for which he received the 2009 Olivier award for Best Theatre Choreography. Other choreography and movement director credits include *365* (National Theatre of Scotland), *Frankenstein* (Royal and Derngate), *Dido Queen of Carthage, The Hothouse* and *Market Boy* (National Theatre, London), *The Bacchae* (National Theatre of Scotland), *The Wolves in the Walls* (National Theatre of Scotland/ Improbable), *Villette* (Stephen Joseph Theatre), *Jerusalem* (West Yorkshire Playhouse), *Mercury Fur* and *The Straits* (Paines Plough).

Steven has recently choreographed the Green Day musical *American Idiot* in the USA.

## Laura Hopkins
*Designer*

Laura's previous work for the National Theatre of Scotland includes *Peter Pan* (with the Barbican), *Black Watch* and *The House of Bernarda Alba*. Recent work for Frantic Assembly includes *Stockholm* and *Othello*.

Current and recent costume designs include *Shoes* (Sadlers Wells), *The Glass Menagerie* (Young Vic); *Juliet and her Romeo* (Bristol Old Vic), *Sinatra* (West End and UK tour) and *Rudolph (*Raimund Theatre, Vienna).

Set and costume designs include *The Merchant of Venice* (Royal Shakespeare Company), *Peer Gynt*, (Tyrone Guthrie Theatre, Minneapolis), *Adolf Hitler, My Part in his Downfall* (Bristol Old Vic and Tour), *The Storm, Dido, Queen of Carthage, The Golden Ass* and *Macbeth* (Shakespeare's Globe), *Kellerman*, (Imitating the Dog), *Time and the Conways* (National Theatre), *Rough Crossings, Faustus* (Headlong), *Othello, Hamlet* and *Faustus* (winner of the 2004 TMA Design award; Northampton), and *Le Compte D'Ory* (Garsington Opera).

## Andy Purves
*Lighting Designer*

Andy trained in Sound and Lighting Engineering at the University of Derby and has an MA in Lighting Design and Theatre-making from the Central School of Speech and Drama, London, where he also tutors in Lighting.

Lighting design projects include: *Stockholm* (Frantic Assembly / Sydney Theatre Company); *Babel* (Stan Won't Dance), *The Erpingham Camp* (Hydrocracker / Brighton Festival), *Ida Barr* and *Office Party* (Barbican), *Frankenstein* (Northampton Royal), *Home Inverness* (National Theatre of Scotland), *Outre* and *Ren-Sa* (Array).

He has also worked with Spymonkey, Company FZ, Tangere Arts, Greenwich and Docklands Festival, Circus Space and on *La Clique* at The Roundhouse and in the West End.

## Carolyn Downing

*Sound Designer*

Carolyn trained at the Central School of Speech and Drama, graduating in 2002 with a 1st class honours degree in Theatre Practice, specialising in Sound Design.

Theatre credits include: *Krieg der Bilder (*Staatstheater Mainz, Germany*), After Dido* (ENO at Young Vic), *Dimetos, Absurdia* (Donmar Warehouse), *All My Sons* (Schoenfeld Theatre, New York), *Tre Kroner - Gustav III* (Dramaten, Sweden), *Angels in America* (Headlong), *The Gods Weep, The Winter's Tale, Pericles, Days of Significance* (Royal Shakespeare Company), *3rd Ring Out* (Metis Arts), *Gambling* (Soho Theatre), *Lulu, The Kreutzer Sonata, Vanya*, *State of Emergency, The Internationalist* (Gate Theatre), *Andersen's English, Flight Path* (Out of Joint), *Oxford Street, Alaska* (Royal Court, London), *A Whistle in the Dark, Moonshed* (Royal Exchange Theatre), *Blood Wedding* (Almeida), *Stallerhof (*Southwark Playhouse), *The Watery Part of the World* (Sound and Fury).


## Ian William Galloway

*Video Designer*

Ian is a video designer and director. He works as part of Mesmer, a collaboration of video and projection designers working in the worlds of theatre, dance, opera, fashion and music.

Theatre credits include *The Lion's Face* (The Opera Group), *The Gods Weep* (Royal Shakespeare Company), *The Kreutzer Sonata, Nocturnal* (Gate Theatre), Medea/ Medea (Headlong), *The Spanish Tragedy* (Arcola), *Proper Clever* (Liverpool Playhouse), *The Tempest* (Lightworks), *Blood* (Royal Court, London), *Starvin'* (Fitzgerald & Stapleton), *Julius Caesar* (Barbican), *A Minute Too Late, Battleship Potemkin* (Complicite), *Hitchcock Blonde* (Alley Theatre, Houston & South Coast Repertory, LA) and *Hôtel de Pékin* (Nationale Reisopera, Netherlands).

Ian has toured as a musician and has designed and directed video for concerts (Leona Lewis, Interpol, RizMC). He also directs music videos and short films.

# Underworld

Underworld is Rick Smith and Karl Hyde. The duo have been making experimental and electronic music together since meeting in Cardiff in 1980. Inspired by the nascent club scene in the UK in the early '90s, Smith and Hyde jettisoned the baggage of the previous decade and began bending and twisting the accepted formula of dancefloor records.

The culmination of this process was their first album, *Dubnobasswithmyheadman*, described at the time by *Melody Maker* as "the most important album since *The Stone Roses* and the best since *Screamadelica*." In the years since, Underworld have successfully balanced critical and commercial success, releasing a string of heavily eulogised albums (*Second Toughest In The Infants*, *Beaucoup Fish*, *A Hundred Days Off* and *Oblivion With Bells*) all the while cementing a reputation as one of the most visceral and inspiring live bands on the planet.

Alongside working together as Underworld, Smith and Hyde are founding partners in the design company Tomato. Their unique visuals have helped lend Underworld records and gigs a distinctive look and feel.

Underworld's long-term relationship with director Danny Boyle saw their track *Born Slippy: Nuxx* used in his adaptation of *Trainspotting*. Clever matching of visuals and music resulted in that track straddling an entire summer in the UK before eventually attaining anthem status only usually afforded to works by stadium rock bands. Smith and Hyde also helped soundtrack Boyle's sci-fi epic *Sunshine*.

Underworld's sixth album, *Barking*, is due for release later in the year. Their first to be recorded with outside studio help, *Barking* finds Underworld working with a carefully selected band of producers and musicians to make their finest record in years.


*Beautiful Burnout* features the music of Underworld

www.underworldlive.com

# *Frantic* assembly

**'14 years of producing superb physical theatre'**
*The Guardian*

Frantic Assembly is celebrated at home and abroad for creating thrilling, energetic and unforgettable theatre. The company attracts new and young audiences with work that reflects contemporary culture. Vivid and dynamic, Frantic Assembly's unique physical style combines movement, design, music and text.

Scott Graham and Steven Hoggett formed Frantic Assembly in 1994. They have since performed in or directed all of the company's work. They seek to collaborate on original ideas with today's most exciting artists. Past collaborators include Bryony Lavery, Hybrid, Laura Hopkins, Abi Morgan, Imogen Heap, Mark Ravenhill and Natasha Chivers.

In addition to its productions Frantic Assembly operates an extensive Creative Learning and Training Programme introducing 5,000 participants a year to the company's process of creating theatre, in a wide variety of settings. Frantic Assembly has recently launched *Ignition,* an innovative vocational training project for young men.

# Productions

| | | |
|---|---|---|
| *Stockholm* | Bryony Lavery | 2010 |
| | *Australian production with Sydney Theatre Company* | |
| *Othello* | William Shakespeare | 2008 |
| *Stockholm* | Bryony Lavery | 2007 |
| *pool (no water)* | Mark Ravenhill | 2006 |
| *Dirty Wonderland* | Michael Wynne | 2005 |
| *On Blindness* | Glyn Cannon | 2004 |
| *Rabbit* | Brendan Cowell | 2003 |
| *Peepshow* | Isabel Wright | 2002 |
| *Heavenly* | Scott Graham, Steven Hoggett and Liam Steel | 2002 |
| *Tiny Dynamite* | Abi Morgan | 2001 |
| *Underworld* | Nicola McCartney | 2000 |
| *Hymns* | Chris O'Connell | 1999 |
| *Sell Out* | Michael Wynne | 1998 |
| *Zero* | Devised by the company | 1997 |
| *Flesh* | Spencer Hazel | 1996 |
| *Klub* | Spencer Hazel | 1995 |
| *Look Back in Anger* | John Osborne | 1994 |

Frantic Assembly have performed, created and collaborated in 28 different countries around the world.

Frantic Assembly is a charity registered in England and Wales 1113716

Supported by
**ARTS COUNCIL ENGLAND**

Scottish theatre has always been for the people, led by great performances, great stories and great writers. As Scotland's national theatre, we exist to work collaboratively with the best companies and individuals to produce and tour world class theatre.

Our ambitions are simple: to create work that excites, entertains and challenges audiences at home and beyond and which makes Scotland proud. We're a theatre company with an adventurous streak and at our heart is a strong desire not to do things conventionally.

Everything we aspire to challenges the notion of what theatre can achieve. With no building of our own we're free to make theatre wherever we can connect with an audience.

For the latest information on all our activity visit our online home at www.nationaltheatrescotland.com

National Theatre of Scotland
Civic House,
26 Civic Street,
Glasgow G4 9RH
T: +44 (0) 141 221 0970
F: +44 (0) 141 331 0589
E: info@nationaltheatrescotland.com

www.nationaltheatrescotland.com

**The National Theatre of Scotland wishes to thank the following individuals and organisations for their support:**

Crerar Hotels
Inchyre Trust
JarHair
Leeds Building Society
Merchants House of Glasgow
Mr Boyd Tunnock
Mrs Katharine Liston
Mr Martin Segal
Miss E.C. Hendry's Charitable Trust
Nancie Massey Charitable Trust
Tayfield Foundation
The Alma and Leslie Wolfson Charitable Trust
The Binks Trust
The Craignish Trust
The Endrick Trust
The Hugh Fraser Foundation
The Pleasance Trust
The RJ Larg Family Trust
The Roger & Sarah Bancroft Clark Charitable Trust
The RS Macdonald Charitable Trust
The Robertson Trust
The Russell Trust
Two Fat Ladies Restaurants
Schuh
ScottishPower
Talteg Limited
Tayfield Foundation
Union Advertising Agency

The National Theatre of Scotland is core funded by the Scottish Government.

The National Theatre of Scotland is a registered Scottish charity SCO33377.

The Scottish
Government

barbican

The **bite** season at the Barbican presents fresh new work that hovers on the very edges of classification. Work that marries dance, theatre and music in unexpected ways, explores what theatre could be, stirs emotions, is passionate, mischievous and makes you smile.

Much of the work that is presented is produced or co-commissioned by bite. It aims to enable the realisation of dreams, encourage ambitious plans and promote the exploration of new ideas. The Barbican is proud to count the **National Theatre of Scotland** amongst its closest partners and collaborators. We are thrilled to be working with **Frantic Assembly** for the first time bringing *Beautiful Burnout* to the iconic York Hall in Bethnal Green.

This November, the National Theatre of Scotland returns to the Barbican with landmark theatrical event, *Black Watch*. Following its outstanding success at the 2009 Olivier Awards this production will feature a brand new cast. To book now for performances 27 Nov 2010–22 Jan 2011, visit barbican.org.uk/bite10 or call the Box Office on 0844 243 0785.

For full details of the new bite10 Sep–Dec season please visit barbican.org.uk/bite10

Barbican Centre, Silk Street,
London, EC2Y 8DS
barbican.org.uk/bite

CITY
OF
LONDON

The City of London
Corporation is the founder
and principal funder
of the Barbican Centre

# Beautiful Burnout 2010

Pleasance Forth, Edinburgh
4 – 29 August
www.pleasance.co.uk

Tramway, Glasgow
2 – 11 September
www.tramway.org

York Hall Leisure Centre, London
(In association with the Barbican)
16 September – 2 October
www.barbican.org.uk

Rothes Halls, Glenrothes
13 – 16 October
www.attfife.org.uk

Crucible, Sheffield
3 - 13 November
www.sheffieldtheatres.co.uk

Minerva Theatre, Chichester
16 – 27 November
www.cft.org.uk

Creative Learning Resources are available for this
production. For further information about the online
resource pack, workshops, master classes and more visit:
www.franticassembly.co.uk

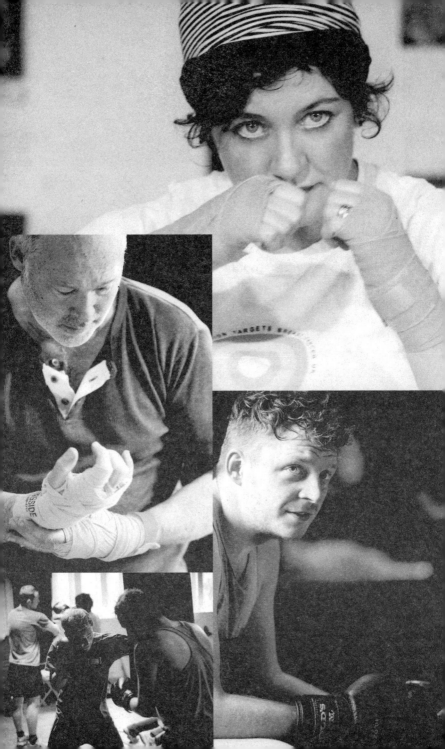

"be comfortable, be subtle, don't chase the air. Don't try to hurt fresh air" Kevin...

Refs only words:
Box.
Rope.
Break.

# Artistic Directors' Note

The idea for *Beautiful Burnout* initially came from a 10 minute visit to Gleason's Gym, a world famous boxing gym in Brooklyn. It's quite hidden, just a doorway on a street. It was about 10 o'clock at night and the sweat, the focus, the smell, the energy, the noise, the intense application was mesmerising. It was one of those moments where you find yourself entering into a world that somehow you knew was there but never had any direct experience of.

We started talking about how to capture this experience within a show, how boxing shows we had seen had never quite presented a credible physicality. We felt inspired by the challenge of giving an audience that same visceral, thrilling and conflicting experience of the visit to Gleason's.

Watching boxing can come with its own moral dilemma. Boxing is often referred to as the "noble art", the "sweet science" by its supporters. It can be idolised and revered by academics and artists but even the people who love and appreciate it can often struggle to defend it morally. The wilful infliction of damage upon an opponent is utterly abhorrent to others and has been considered a blood sport. There is a massive range of responses and reaction here. There's an incredible tension between those two points of view. That tension became really interesting for us to start grappling with.

Boxing is a provocative subject. We had no intention of shying away from the moral debate surrounding boxing. It is this debate that convinced us we had something to say about this world. The issue of how damage is both present and buried within a sport that appears to offer its participant's support, focus, and discipline is fascinating to both of us.

In researching the Scottish boxing world we have found people who dedicate their time and energies to others, people who find a home in boxing, in its camaraderie, its positive role models, its ethos of discipline and respect. We have been welcomed at every stage by people interested in what we were doing and keen to help in any way they can. We have to thank the people who generously opened this world up to us. Danny Lee in Greenock and Terry McCormack in Edinburgh have inspired and informed our work. Kevin Smith has shown the patience of a saint as he guided us through boxing technique and strategy.

This show was always going to ask a lot of its cast. We have put them through a rigorous training regime and they have taken to it with gusto. Inspired by the positivity and support palpable within boxing gyms, they have encouraged and pushed each other at every stage. We owe this cast more than we could ever express here. They are a source of inspiration for us. We have never had so much sweat in a rehearsal room. Or outside of it.

We are about to enter our final week of rehearsal and are still working on the text with Bryony. It has been an intense and lengthy process that goes some way to demonstrating just how dedicated and unrelenting Bryony has been in getting this right. It's a world that is difficult to represent without falling into cliché but we believe that the text we have here celebrates and represents this world with honesty and integrity.

Scott Graham and Steven Hoggett
July 2010

## *Beautiful Burnout*
## Scenes and Tracklisting

$( B.B^{v.} 8 )$     July '10

♪

Morning        please help me
Food Chain
Ref #1        Hungerford Bridge
Gym Enter
2 Hours        No More
Fighting Fist       Ancient Phat Farm
Wraps #1       Glam Bucket
Clocks / Scribble / Star    Scribble / ?? Old Film ??
Zanussi       Showlder
Dina School
Spar
Cheese Fridge
Amateurs
Bobby's Eyes
Kitten! / Catch Up Pads    Kitten! / Bird
Promotion        ↓
Fridge Head
Get Yer Kit       ??
Ever
Handcream
Dina Space      River of Bass
2 Ajays       Monkey 2
Breath
Arrested / E      Dub Shepherd
Menace       Simple Pear
Wraps #2 / Refs / Spearmint   Geeze
Fight        Beautiful Burnout
Beautiful Burnout     ??
Ref #2       Exam ?
One Punch      Carlton !
Black Lights      To Bed

⟨post ... Diamond Jigsaw? Coughin?⟩

*Finale's*
Ford A Ready
Boy³
Geeze (encore)

**Bryony Lavery**

Beautiful Burnout

*faber and faber*

First published in 2010
by Faber and Faber Limited
74–77 Great Russell Street
London WC1B 3DA

Typeset by Country Setting, Kingsdown, Kent CT14 8ES
Printed in England by CPI Bookmarque, Croydon, Surrey

A CIP record for this book is available from the British Library

ISBN 978-0-571-27359-1

2 4 6 8 10 9 7 5 3 1

# Characters

*in order of appearance*

**Ajay Chopra**
a boxer

**Cameron Burns**
a boxer

**Ainsley Binnie**
a boxer

**Neil Neill**
a boxer

**Dina Massie**
a boxing lassie

**Carlotta**
a boxer's mother

**Steve George**
a referee

**Bobby Burgess**
a boxing trainer

The odd line lengths
weird          spacing
and plethora of exclamation marks
and question marks in the text
are the author's attempt to convey
the frenetic nature of these characters
in their situation!!!

/ in the text indicates one character
talking over another

## SOME DICTIONARY DEFINITIONS

**Time,** *noun.* A limited stretch or space of continued existence, as the interval between two successive events or acts, or the period through which an action, condition, or state continues . . .

**Beautiful,** *adjective.* Very pleasing and impressive to listen to, touch, or especially to look at; very good or enjoyable.

**Burnout,** *noun.* Psychological exhaustion and diminished efficiency resulting from overwork or prolonged exposure to stress; somebody affected by psychological exhaustion. [*Informal.*] Failure of a machine or part of a machine to work because of overuse and excessive heat or friction; failure of a rocket or jet engine to work because the fuel supply has been exhausted or cut off.

# BEAUTIFUL BURNOUT

We are always in and around a boxing ring.

Life is what happens in the few moments in, during, around the obsessive path towards becoming the brightest star in the night sky . . .

We are in a world of freely shared opinions and self-promotion . . .

# ONE
## A REFEREE PREPARES

*The early hours of morning.*
*Steve George: intent, intensely focused on a screen . . .*
*He has a remote control . . . screens.*
*He might be a night security guard . . .*
*He might work in Currys . . .*
*He's in an entirely self-imagined future documentary,*
STEVE GEORGE – THE REFEREE'S REFEREE, *in which a referee watches himself on YouTube . . . He's both voice-over* and *modest interviewee.*

**Steve**
He's refereeing impeccably . . .
Steve George
This seasoned professional . . .
This much-respected referee . . .

His job
Is to
Watch *like an eagle*
And 'protect the boxer without fear or favour' . . .
And this Steve George is a
Fucking beady-eyed fucking *golden* eagle!

(*He watches like a fucking beady-eyed fucking golden eagle . . .*
*His body starts to channel the body movements of what he is doing on screen.*)

He calls it.
There's a Winner
There's a Loser

Everyone's safe in the hands of this man.

Let's see that *again*, Boxing Aficionados!

(*And presses replay . . .*)

## TWO
### FOOD RUNS IN OUR FAMILY

*A washing machine churning . . .*
  *Carlotta, very near the ring . . .*
  *She's just putting a load in.*
  *It's early. It's not domestic.*

**Carlotta**
  Welcome to the glamour of boxing!
  Who *is* that Mysterious Figure loading the Zanussi???
  Human Beings call me Carlotta . . .
  But . . .
  Under the *umbrella* title of *Mother*
  I'm
  Headcookcleanerbottlewasher*launderette*alarmclock
  Small investment-vulnerable-lending-bank-with-over-
  generous-overdraft-facilities . . .
  *Bulk* combiner of proteincarbsroughage
  Calorie supplier

  I *feed* The Beast.

  (*Selects a programme.*)

  Food runs in our family.
  My nan was dinner lady up at St Paul's
  My dad worked at Tunnock's
  My ex-husband *ate* food
  My son *eats* food
  I *cook* it
  See how *that* works?

*Presses a power button.*

The only time my son doesnae eat *my* food
Is when he's on his two-week junkfood binge after a
fight . . .
FishandchipsKFCMcDonald'sdeepfriedMarsbars
OhYes
All doon that mighty gullet into that ceaseless digestive
system
He's a taste for rubbish which he inherited from his
*father*

who now eats at another address

courtesy of a *Skank* name of Sheila Diver!

Skank!
Skank Shagger! . . .

Move *on*
*Closure.*

Otherwise
At *this* eatery   it's
Mince and tatties Monday
Steak pie Tuesday
Liver and bacon Wednesday
Thursday beef stew with carrots and onions oh *yes*!
Spaghetti bolognese I'm multi-cultural Friday
Saturday he's oot
Sunday roast dinner who makes the best roast
potatoes in *the world*
*I* make the best roast potatoes in the world!!!
Breakfast today is

*And she's getting . . .*

*Four* boiled eggs   toast   and   jelly beans . . .

*Jelly beans*!!!

Eggs boiled for *three* minutes no more, 'Like three
minutes in boxing, Mum, nae mare nae less,' the
*Future Champion* likes his eggs 'jest soft enough tae
dip ma soldiers in!'
Three minutes 'nae mare nae less' it is.

(*And a clock times . . .*

*Sings.*)

'Ti  i  i ime
is on ma side
yes it is . . .'

(*To some slow water.*) Boil.

My son sees me as quite *far* doon the food chain . . .
It goes
Famous Boxers Alive Or Dead
Any Boxers
Anybody who isnae a boxer still but knows anything
about boxing
Males
Fit Lassies
Lassies
Dogs
Cartoon Characters
Me

(*To some slow water that's still not.*) I said *boil.*

No kidding    *jelly beans* for breakfast!
'Jelly beans is for energy'
Is that insane?    Aye
Is ma son insane?    Aye
Am I insane???
Hold that thought!

(*And water boils.*
    *Eggs cook.*)

## THREE
## A SPLIT SECOND

*Dark still.*
  *Bobby Burgess, a boxing trainer: keys to . . .*
  *Unlock    reveal*
  *Some harsh unnatural light to cut the darkness . . .*
  *A space for us . . .*
  *Sign:* BOBBY BURGESS BOXING
  *He's just off a night shift, he's dog tired.*

**Bobby**
  You pretend
  It's fifteen minutes half an hour one investigative
  session tops
  Before
  You know whether a lad's a boxer or not . . .
  You watch them
  Give them instructions
  See if they listen
  See if they can learn.

  (*He starts setting up . . . Finding punchbags, whatever,
  in the bellies of washing machines, skipping ropes
  drawn from Hoovers . . .*)

  You say
  'I'll watch you
  See your style, I'll know in fifteen minutes'
  But
  You're lying
  Actually
  It takes aboot five seconds . . .

  (*He continues setting up.*)

  No
  Lying again

You know in a second
No
A *split* second
You've struck gold
Hit pay dirt
Found that rich seam
Dug up a *born* boxer        Eureka

He's called Ajay Chopra
He's a wee brun lad from Paisley
Already
He's subtle he's quick
He doesnae try to hurt fresh air . . .
He's the best lad at this stage I've ever seen . . .

But    you keep *that* to *yourself*
Because . . .
Finding one's the easy part
Making one fulfil his promise?
Another story *altaegether!* . . .
They're all bloody silly testosteroned *teenagers*
Daft wee skelfs who think they know *everything* . . .
The section of society that knows the *least*
But believes they know *everything*
And therefore have minds *programmed* to *kibosh*
Any chance of personal success . . .

(*He tries to hoist the punchbag onto its hook. It is very heavy . . .*)

What do you do?

Try make them listen to *Reason*???

Wake Up!

Expect *Sense*???

Dream On!

You fucking *frighten* them

*Boo!!!*

Reign of *Terror*

(*He punches . . .*)

Do as I say!

(*Everything does as he says.*)

Who rules the world?

*I* rule the world!

(*The world does as he says,*

*Everything obeys him . . . even the lights which –*)


## FOUR
### TWO HOURS, TWICE A WEEK

*– go on full and:*
  *We're in the glory of the gym, where Bobby Bobby –*
*God of the Universe, King Bobby – commands . . . reigns.*
  *It's the junior training session with junior boxers: Ajay*
*Chopra, Ainsley Binnie, Dina Massie and Neil Neill . . .*

**Bobby**
  Let's go, lads, let's go let's see you kill it.

  (*All intently focused on young men/girl training.*)

  It's your *shoulder* carries your guard

  Raise your guard
  Raise your guard
  Open your body
  And close it

  Remember . . .
  Your jaw's connected to your legs!

Stay outside the distance
Stay outside the distance
Watch your man
Watch your *man!!!*

You're under *constant surveillance*
I'm watching you
Auld Alec's watching you, so's Dougie
Whammo's watching you, so's Young Alec

It's *two* hours
*Twice* a week
In these two hours
Ye work as *hard* as ye can
As *much* as ye can!

**All**

Yes, Mr Burgess!

**Bobby**

No talking keep your breath for *boxing*!

Keep your balance at all times
Walking
Nice and relaxed nice and relaxed

Let your bones carry you

(*They let their bones carry them.*)

Slip to the inside
Slip to the outside

Step inside

Good

(*Cameron enters. Not in gear. Watches it all.*)

It's your ability to make people *miss*
Think all your wee moves, guys
Think your combinations, lads

Don't hold back you're only cheating yourself

(*To Cameron.*) In a minute, laddie . . .

(*Cameron stands . . .*)

**Bobby**
Be *comfortable*    be *subtle*
Don't chase the air
Don't try to hurt fresh air
That's no who you're trying to beat

Good.

(*A bell goes and a temporary lull in training and sound.*)

*One* minute!

Alright, lads . . . take your wee sips . . .
You too, lassie . . .
Dinnae get dehydrated . . .

(*Knackered, they get their water bottles.*)

See my eyes

(*They all see his eyes . . .*)

Wherever *you* are, *they* are
And I never sleep
They never close
I'm *watching* you
I'm seeing you
Whammo's prowling
Dougie's beading you
The Two Alecs have you in a *crossbeam* of concentration

*Wee* sips!

(*They take* wee *sips.*)

Your *rests* are important

(*They all nod.*)

Keep your minds switched *on*
I *know* when you switch off in there
These eyes can see into your brains . . .

(*They believe him.*)

(*To Cameron.*) Can I help you?

**Cameron**
I want to be one of these

The best one

**Bobby**
Everyone wants to be 'the best one'
*Right*, lads?

**Ajay/Neil/Ainsley/Dina**
Right, Mr Burgess!

**Bobby**
And lassie.
This is our *Million Dollar Baby* . . .
Say 'Hello' to . . .?

**Cameron**
Cameron    Burns

**Ajay/Neil/Ainsley**
Alright?

**Cameron**
Alright.

You train lassies?

**Bobby**
We train *this* one.

You got a problem with that?

**Cameron**
No    no problem. (*Untrue.*)

**Dina**  (*perfect, if slightly exaggerated imitation*)
'No   no problem.'

(*Fairly quietly.*) Wanker.

**Bobby**
Alright
Alright
Your minute's *up*
Good timekeeping's *essential*

Water bottles *doon*

(*He concentrates on Cameron.*)

Okay, laddie

(*He does mime: 'Eyes on me.'*)

Eyes on me
Eyes *always* on me
That's the way to *catch up* with these other numpties

(*They all grin . . . to be called a numpty by King Bobby, big accolade.*)


### FIVE
### A FIGHTING FIST LANDS
### A HUNDRED PUNCHES IN THREE MINUTES

*Bobby demonstrates to Cameron . . .*
*The assorted numpties probably show they know too.*

**Bobby**
It's *simple.*
A fighting fist lands a hundred punches per three-
minute round
You want to land as many punches

Per round as you can
Good punches means *points*
Calzaghe averaged nine-fifty tae a thousand per *match*
And that's what wears your opponent doon
It's what *wins*
You want to do it *right*!

(*He lifts his hand into the air.*)

Your hand's *delicate*
It contains twenty-seven bones

(*Everybody lifts their hands into the air.*)

Striking a blow incorrectly can cause serious / damage

Develop a safe and solid punching fist

**Ainsley**
Carpals    *meta* carpals, right? Mr Burgess . . .

**Neil Neill** (*as he puts two fingers up at Ainsley Binnie*)
I've only got two bones in mine . . .

**Ajay**
Shut the fuck *up*, you moronic fuck / wit . . .

**Bobby**
*Excuse me???*

**Ajay/Ainsley/Neil**
Sorry, Mr Burgess /

**Bobby**
Curl your fingers

(*Cameron also curls his fingers.*)

Tuck the tips in the middle of your palm
Fold your thumb over your fingers so
It doesnae stick out beyond the line of your knuckles
Your fist should be lightly clenched

(*Everyone makes a fist.*)

Until
Impact.

(*Everyone makes impact in the air.*)

Punch in a straight line
It travels in a straight line
From the shoulder

(*It is beautiful.*)

The fist turns
Inward before impact
So only the flat knuckle part hits the target

(*The human body is truly amazing . . .*)

This locks oot the arm

(*To Ajay.*) Show him

**Ajay** (*demonstrates*)
The fist turns
Inward before impact
So only the flat knuckle part hits the target
This locks oot the arm

(*Cameron watches Ajay.*)

And rounds the shoulder
To protect the chin . . .

**Bobby**
Well remembered that, Chopra

Good.

**Ajay** (*to Cameron*)
Four types of attack.
The hook

(*They both hook.*)

The jab

(*They both jab.*)

**Bobby** (*to Cameron*)
Good

**Ajay**
Straight punch

(*Straight punch.*)

To the head
To the body

Uppercut

(*They uppercut.*)

To the body
To the chin
Your target area is any point on the front or sides of
the head or body
Above the belt.

(*Cameron puts the different punches together in a fast
combination . . .*)

**Bobby** (*to Cameron*)
Good

(*To us.*) You know in a second
Born boxer.

**Ajay**
Born boxer, Bobby
No as pretty a colour as *me* though . . .

**Bobby**
No *cheek*, you.
There'll be no *colour* prejudice in *my* gym
Nothing wrong with bright *pink* . . .
Okay

I've had enough of your splendour for noo
Get oot of my hair.

**Neil Neill**
What hair, Mr Burgess?

(*He looks at them.*)

Going, Mr Burgess.

(*And they all vaporise.*)

(*To Cameron.*) No you.

Stay.


SIX
WELCOME TO MY STRANGE PLANET

*He dresses his new male baby . . .*
*Equips him for a new planet . . .*

**Bobby**
This is *your* planet noo, Cameron Burns.
This is where *your* species survive.
Your DNA thrives in this rarefied atmosphere.

**Cameron**
Alright. (*Whatever . . .*)

**Bobby**
This here's the last free gift you'll get from me.

(*From somewhere secret he finds hand bandages.*)

Either yourself
Or somebody stupid enough to care aboot you

**Cameron**
My dad . . . my mum's as tight as a nun's / fanny

23

**Bobby**

Dinnae interrupt . . . needs tae get you
gloves bandages vests shorts warmup warmdoon gear
boots    ask *Ajay*   the *brun* laddie?    what's best to get
head guard a good one tae protect what brains you've
got in your head . . .

**Cameron**

Teachers say I've nae brains in there anyway . . .

**Bobby**

Do they?
Well . . . lucky for *you* . . .
*I'll* be your brains for you!
Every Tuesday and Friday
Six p.m.
Sharp
Two hours twice a week
Nae latecomers
Nae fly-by-night I don't feel like it tonight I want tae
watch
Feckin *Strictly-EastEnders*!!!

**Cameron**

Aye    alright

**Bobby**

You need to look after these
They're your precision instruments.

(*Bobby bandages his hands for him . . . as . . .*)

This is a piece of Good Luck
That I've handed you
We don't get given a big bag full of luck
People like us
An infinitesimally small few of us
Get
One little piece
Don't expect any more

24

Grab it
Grab your *one* piece of luck
This is your chance, Cameron Burns

**Cameron**
Aye   alright

**Bobby**
Make your parents proud of you

*Much* more important . . .

Make me proud of you

**Cameron**
*Ontae* it!

**Bobby**
Put 'em *up*!

(*Cameron puts up his now bandaged hands. Bobby
adjusts them for him.*)

Up.

(*And he's in stance as . . .*

*The other young boxers return on the bell.*)


SEVEN
EVEN THE CLOSEST STAR TAKES
FOUR YEARS FOR ITS LIGHT TO REACH US

*They're ready . . .*

**Bobby**
Okay
Let's get doon tae business!

(*And he sets up . . .*)

See *this*?

(*A clock face . . . a timer . . .*)

That's *your* face now.
That's the machinery what's ticking inside your brain.
You're all Human Clocks
From now on, you'll be living your life in three-minute bursts
From now on, you're no made up of flesh and bone . . .
You're made of *minutes*
Your minutes are made ae *seconds*
In which you need tae move and think faster than the speed of light.
Seconds full of *activity* and    *choices*

(*He takes them to . . .*)

You need tae keep your clock *ticking* so
Let's set you in perpetual motion

(*He places them . . . shows them . . .*)

Burpies    like *this*
Here

Press-ups
Here

Sit-ups
Here

Star jumps    *full* stretch
Here

One minute of your valuable time on each one
Full commitment
Clocks
Start ticking
Go!

(*And they are in 'timing' time.*
   *Ajay, Neil Neill, Ainsley, Cameron and Dina perform each type for a minute, then move to another, as Bobby, and the clock, times them . . .*

*They also try to turn from raw human bodies into the
stars of myth and legend . . .*
    *This will not yet be possible.*)

**Ainsley**
In the red corner
Ainsley Binnie!

**Ajay**
In the blue corner . . .

Ajay Chopra!

**Neil Neill**
And in the red corner!
Neil Neill!

**Ainsley**
The Man to Watch
The Name to Know
The dangerously effective
The fabulously gifted
Ainsley Binnie!

**Ajay**
Ajay Chopra!

Ajay    '*Unconquerable*'!

Chopra    'The Cobra . . . the *Spitting* Cobra'!

**Neil Neill**
Let me introduce you to this new name in boxing
This name to watch!
Neil Neill!
So good, they named him twice!

**Ajay** (*which sounds better?*)
The Puncher from Paisley . . .?
The Punjabi Jabber . . .?

The Asian *Invasion*!

**Neil Neill**
Neill makes his opponents *kneel* before him!

Neil Neill 'Fists of steel'!

**Dina**
Can't believe I'm *participating* in this . . .
Okay . . .
Dina Massie
The Battling Lassie
Dina Massie . . .
'Tits of Terror'

**Ainsley**
Ainsley Binnie
A rounded *renaissance* man
Unusual in a boxer he's something of a *bookworm*
Interests
Martial arts
Astronomy
And the history of sword dancing
The *Amazing* Ainsley Binnie!

(*Chatting up Dina.*) Did you know . . . actually . . .
Dina . . .
Scottish dancing started as essentially pugilistic . . .
Fact.

**Dina** (*lying*)
Interesting

**Ajay**
Ajay Chopra
Excellence Acumen Technique *Television*!

(*And they are all on star jumps.*)

**Ainsley**
A Future Star!

**Ajay**
The brightest star

**Neil Neill**
Neil Neill
Look!
Even his *body's* star-shaped!

(*Bobby, returned, watches them get lax. It doesn't please him.*)

**Ainsley**
Astronomy-wise . . .
A star is a massive, luminous ball of plasma held together by gravity?
Fact.

**Neil Neill**
I know *you're* a massive luminous ball of *shite* held together by gravity
Fact.

**Dina**
Shut it, Fists ae Fuck

(*He shuts it.*)

**Ajay**
A Shooting Star!
From the East
Racing across the Western Sky . . .

**Cameron**
Cameron     Burns
Cameron 'Serious' Burns . . .?

**Neil Neill**
No, not good. No!!!

**Cameron**
Cameron     'Third Degree' Burns . . .?

**Neil Neill**
No!!!

**Cameron**

Cameron Burns 'Fists of Fury'.

**Neil Neill**

We cannae both be 'Fists'
You need to be something else . . .
I was 'Fists' first
We can't both be fists.

**Ainsley** (*still seductively, to Dina*)

Actually     Dina

Even the closest star takes four years for the *light alone* to reach us.

**Dina**

Go away

**Ainsley**

Fact

**Dina**

Right away

(*Ainsley goes away.*)

Just for future reference
*This*    is how much space I require around me!!!
Watch me streak across the sky!
I'm wind I'm sleet I'm storm I'm black clouds
I'm the worst weather front you'll ever meet!
Don't fuckincome near me...
Don't fuckinthinkaboutit!
I'll pull your balls off and stuff them doon your gawpingaspinthroat so you can have them for breakfast!!!
I'll kill you!
Now
Fuck *off* Out of My Space You Fucking Fannies!

(*And she establishes her own personal space.
And she's back in . . .*)

**Boys**
Fucking *Star*!

That's ME!!!

(*Bobby comes back in command.*)

**Bobby**
That's *who???*

(*They try to be very unnoticeable.*)

*Youse* lot???

Dream *on*!

What makes a star?
What makes you earthbound blobs of shite intae a
glittering star in the boxing firmament???
Hard bloody graft!
It takes four bloody years before youse lot's light
reaches us!
*Fact!!!*
Who made the stars?
Who made the universe?
Who???

**All**
God!

**Bobby**
Who's God?

**Boys/Dina**
You are!

**Bobby**
I'm *God*. Who am I?

**Boys/Dina**
God!

**Bobby**

I'm *King Robert*
King Robert    *The Bruise!*
Who Am I?

**Boys/Dina**

King Robert    *The Bruise!!!*

**Bobby**

You obey *my* discipline
You follow all *my* rules

(*He's physically correcting stances, attitudes as . . .*)

You practise *my* good behaviour
I teach you *my* moves
So you come to no harm if *I* can help it
That's what it's all aboot
Any *stars'll* be up there because *I've* made them
*Twinkle!!!*

(*The universe is all made by him.*)


### EIGHT
### A BOXER'S STAFF: PART ONE

*Carlotta, already with a big pile of boy-washing, journeys the space somehow, collecting any other pieces of boy-washing.*

**Carlotta**

Which soap powder would you recommend
For the removal of sweat?

and    blood    ???

oh aye *blood*
roll up roll up
come watch your lad

magically turn black and blue
see someone change his face frae 'handsome' tae 'Shrek'
watch his ears blossom intae cauliflowers . . .

'You're letting your son participate in a dangerous
sport, Missus???'
'How can you *live* with yourself???'

In my defence, your honour . . .
What I have is
A wain with more energy than the National Grid!
The school said 'He's got a lot ae    *spirit,* Missus
I say, 'Tell me aboot it'
I said, 'Is he being *picked* on?'
School said, 'He's *daeing* the picking!'
I said, 'Oh no! . . . Is he picking on the younger boys?'
They said, 'No, he's picking on the teachers!!!'
I tried putting him under house arrest . . . but
He was oot the window, ontae the veranda dripping
onto the back green
And away intae the shadows . . .

He's *Houdini!*

Nae locks or chains keep this boy in!

At least noo I know where he is

(*Looks at controls.*)

Zanussi    Do you have a programme for 'nosebleeds,
heavy' . . .?

Didn't think so!!!

(*They don't.*
   *She selects a wash programme . . .*
   *She exits next-task direction.*)

## NINE
### DINA DINA, NO ONE'S MEANER

*Dina needs to straighten us out on . . .*

**Dina**

You can wipe that 'What the fuck's *she* daeing there?'
off your faces.

*School* said
'You're a *little* bit oot o control, Dina dear, why *is* that?'
'Fuck off!'

They said, 'Try Tennis!
*You* clearly like *smashing* and *lobbing* stuff, Dina
Massie!'
Fuck off!
They said, 'A lot of the girls like to learn dance!'
If I want tae dance I'll go tae a fucking *club*. Fuck off!
They said, 'What aboot *Drama*?
I want you to improvise a scene with Carleeen where
you're trying to tell your mother you might be
*pregnant* . . .'
Fuck off!
They said, 'Try *Citizenship*!
It's a *sitting-down-quietly* subject and *you* like a good
argument, Dina . . .
You could voice your opinions in a structured
environment . . .'
Fuck        off!
Well then . . . Hmmm? . . . Okay! . . .
Try After-School *Tai Chi*, Dina . . .
You need to *calm down*.
Would you like to investigate *tranquillity*?'
Would you like to investigate 'fuck off?'
Find me something else!

(*And Bobby is there . . .*)

## TEN
## GOOD BOXING AND BAD BOXING

*Bobby watching Dina boxing shadows, Ajay and Ainsley sparring . . .*

**Bobby**
Good

Good.

Be subtle

Don't hurt the air . . .

**Dina**
Air's all I get tae / hurt . . .

**Bobby**
Then why don't you
Go to *women's* boxing . . .?

**Dina**
I don't want to do *women's* boxing
I want to do *boxing*

**Bobby**
Then stop *nagging*
And *do* boxing!

Move, lassie

(*Pushes Dina aside to reach Ajay.*)

Ajay Chopra . . . stop *showboating*!!

You're *boxing*!

**Ajay**
Right.

**Bobby**
No *acting the bloody clown!!!*

**Ajay**
Right . . .
But . . . see . . . if I do this . . .

(*Showboating . . . clowning . . .*)

I invite him to come to me . . .
I piss him off . . .
He loses it . . .
I challenge him to take doon the clown . . .
I *appear* to be open to him . . . but . . .
Meanwhile . . . I get to watch him . . . see where *he's*
going to punch . . .
And effectively *counter* punch . . .

(*And he lands a very good arrested punch on Bobby's
chin . . . which is uber-irritating.*)

And he's doon

What do you think?

(*Bobby holds him, talks to his face . . .*)

**Bobby**
Listen to me
Listen to me
Do what I *say*.
What I *say*.
Your last few seconds there . . .
That's when your opponent
Is most dangerous to you
When you're tired
That's when there's most *blood*, boy!
So you *mind* that!

**Ajay**
But . . .

Here's my point . . . Bobby . . .
It's also when *I'm* most dangerous to my opponent

Because I've made him underestimate me!

I *win*.

**Bobby**
But not in a good way.

**Ajay**
Good boxers are *liars*, Bobby.
We promise one thing, deliver another

**Bobby**
Good boxers *box*, Ajay.
We *box* well.
Will you remember that?

**Ajay**
I remember everything.

**Bobby**
You're an *elephant*, are you???

**Ajay**
I'm a *cobra*
I'm a *champion*

**Bobby**
You're a champion when *I* say you're a champion
(*To Ajay's retreating back.*) Who's God?

(*A beat before . . .*)

**Ajay**
You are, Bobby.

**Bobby**
Who do you *listen* to . . .?

**Ajay**
*You*, King Bobby . . . I listen to *you* . . .

*Carlotta: washing, chugging . . .*

**Carlotta**
Look . . .
You got to do *something* with your wain apart from
Keeping him wrapped up in cotton wool in a box at
the back of your wardrobe . . .
Which would be *my* ideal choice . . .

Listen . . .

It's *amateur* boxing
That's low-level risk and . . .
He's learning
Tae defend himself
Tae learn skills
Tae learn self-control . . . Please God.

*She looks in her fridge.*

Where the bloody hell's the . . .?

(*Shouts up.*) Ho
Mister Light Welterweight!!!???

Have you been in my fridge???

(*Listens.*) I *needed* that cheese!

(*Nobody there . . .*)

O course, the doon side is
He isnae here, he's never here, he's always at
'Training! Okayalrightyeah Jeezus!!'

He's composed entirely oot of testosterone
*Cuddlin* him . . .
It was like holding a big lit *firework* . . .

You *knew* it was going tae go off
You *just* never knew when . . .
Or    no   one of those big stripy tomcats that live
wild   in *sheds*
He'd be up over your shoulder and doon yer back and
off! Before ye could get hold of him . . .

Just like that Skank Shagger of a bloody father . . .

(*And, her kitchen running like clockwork, she's off.*)

So, Your Honour,
So   Gentlemen of the Jury
(a) I know where he is!
(b) I know what he's doing
(c) It's going as well as it can when there's teenage
hormones flying aboot!

Best course of action
Best decision
Best place for him oh yes
Defence rests

But what, I hear you ask yourself . . .
Does this experienced operator of Zanussi and
Hotpoint
Do for fun?

Walk this way!

(*Exits for . . .*)


### TWELVE
### AMATEUR TIME

*The gym . . .*

**Bobby**
Okay   soon   ye'll be fighting other lads from other
clubs

Ye need to know how that works . . .
Ainsley Binnie and Neil Neill will show us how *they*
think it should go . . .
The rest of us is attentive crowd . . .

(*Dina and Ajay watch. Cameron with economy crisp bag.*)

**Cameron**  (*to Ajay*)
Crisp?

**Ajay**
No!

**Cameron**  (*to Dina*)
Crisp?

**Dina**
No!

**Cameron**  (*to Bobby*)
Crisp, Bobby?

(*Bobby snatches the packet from Cameron.*)

**Bobby**
What's *this*???

**Cameron**
Crisps.

**Bobby**
Can't hear you

**Cameron**
Crisps.

**Bobby**
Can't hear you . . .?

(*Waits until Cameron gets it. It may take some time.*)

**Cameron**
Junk, Bobby.

**Bobby**
    *Junk*, Twat
    Ajay . . .?

**Ajay**
    Food's Fuel Energy Potential

**Bobby**
    Listen and Learn, Twat

    (*He throws the crisps away . . .*)

**Dina**
    Twat!

**Bobby**
    You will be holding their little hands through all their
    amateur fights . . .

    (*Neil Neill and Ainsley Binnie in gear, headguards, put
    in their gumshields.
        Because of the gumshields, the following is
    completely incomprehensible . . .*)

**Neil Neill**
    Bobby . . . did you put me in the blue corner or the red
    corner only I cannae remember . . . I was in the blue
    corner in Lanark but I was in the red corner in
    Kirkcaldy . . .

    I think it was the blue corner

    No wait a minute . . .

    I think it was the *red* corner . . .

    Bobby . . .

**Ainsley**
    Bobby . . . will you check this chin strap because the
    other lads have been messing with my kit and I think
    it's got loose and possibly dangerous . . .

And some monkey's put bubble gum in my boots again
and I think it was *either* Cameron Burns *or* Neil
bloody Neill . . .

Bobby

**Bobby**
Idiot Boys   listen to me.

**Both**
Yes, Bobby?

**Bobby**
Anything you want to say to anybody before a match
You have to say *before* you put your gumshields in . . .

Okay?

**Neil/Ainsley**
Yes Bobby sorry Bobby didn't think Bobby

**Bobby**
Okay . . . hoodies off . . .

(*They struggle to take off their warm-up hoodies in
their gloves . . .*)

**Bobby**
And    anything you need to accomplish *before* you
put your gloves on . . .

**Neil/Ainsley**
God, yes . . . good thinking, Bobby . . .

**Bobby**
Go to your corners, Twats.

(*They are in opposite corners.
    Carlotta appears.*)

**Carlotta** (*to us*)
Well, where did you *think* I was going?
Bingo?

The Life of a Boxer's Mother is about
Boxing
Boxing
And . . . (*She demonstrates boxing.*)

(*Bell goes . . .*)

**Bobby**
'And it's Ainsley Binnie frae the Bobby Burgess Gym
fighting
Neil Neill also
Frae the Bobby Burgess Gym!
What a Nurturer o' Young Talent this man is!'

(*They come towards each other for one minute of . . .*)

Ye have to train a lot of toads
To find a boxing prince . . .

(*They fight.*)

Most amateur contests . . .
It's like watching a coupla *hares* in a field . . .

(*We see this wonderful attack and energy . . . but with
terrible, terrible flailing and missing.*
    *With Carlotta, plus Bobby, shouting . . . it becomes
a match with four people . . . two boxers, Carlotta and
Bobby.*)

**Carlotta** (*to us*)
First time I watched this . . .
I just wanted to *burst into tears*!
All these Beautiful Young Boys!
Now
I'm an Extra in
Bloody *Gladiator*!

(*Back to . . .*)

Raise your guard

Your jaw's connected to your legs!

**Bobby**

Surprise! Not Power!

You see how safe it is?

**Carlotta**

Then I realise . . .

**Bobby/Carlotta**

Nobody hits anybody!

**Carlotta**

Keep your balance at all times
Walking
Nice and relaxed nice and relaxed

(*To us.*) After a couple of visits . . .
I get to absolutely bloody *love*
Nice and loose
Slip bang punch
Slip to the inside
Slip to the outside
Step inside now
Good!

**Bobby**

You want to be champions?
You want to be pros?

**Carlotta**

And
I get it
I get why he loves it . . .
It gets into you . . .
It's as good as sex     and no so *complicated*.

(*Bell for the end of the bout.*)

You can see them all get . . . *brighter*

There's     like     a smile in their     bodies . . .

*(They are both high on endorphins.)*

**Neil Neill**
  Magic!!!

**Ainsley**
  When a nerve impulse reaches the spinal chord . . .
  *Endorphins* are released
  Which stop the nerve cells from releasing more pain
  signals
  It allows the body to feel a sense of power
  And have control over itself
  Fact.

*(The boys and Dina group round Bobby.)*

**Carlotta**
  'Endorphins'  *weird* word right?
  in my head
  I always get this *picture*
  the *end* of the world
  Far far away
  And in   sparkling sea . . .
  *dolphins*

  *Mental* . . . right?

*(As she exits on another task . . .)*

  She goes
  She with her endolphins . . .
  See you, boys.

*(Nobody says goodbye to her.*
   *It's not clear which one is her son . . .*
   *And she's off.)*

*They know Bobby's all-seeing eyes are everywhere . . . so
they all go about their business. Boxing is in their DNA in
the boring repetitive tasks/jobs in the outside world as . . .*

**Bobby**

It needs tae be relentless
Ye need tae be *relentless*
Because
In the no sae *salubrious* parts o' different toons . . .
No just Greenock! No just Arbroath Forgewood
Wellmeadow Kirkintilloch
No just Sleigh Drive Edinburgh
There's gyms *everywhere*
Where's lads are waiting tae punch *you*!

**Cameron**

Things I give up for this.
Shoplifting.
Borrowing cars.
Smoking. Tobacco *and* weed.
*Girlfriends.*
I still dae *Shagging* . . .
But only on Friday and Saturday.
I jest cannae dae the *Commitment* Thing wi lassies.

What else . . .???

Crisps.

Spare time.

Spare time . . .
Whit's *that?*

**Bobby**

Just make a few more sacrifices
Just give more time

Because in the East End of London
In the Bloody East End of *Europe* Ukraine Latvia
Georgia
Fucking 'All-Star Gym, Hackensack New Jersey'
Fucking 'Golden Child Boxing Gym, Mandalingong
City'
Lads are getting fitter faster tae fucking fight *you*
luckily for *you*
In the luxurious surroundings
of a wee made-over scout hut in Glamorous Glasgow
Bobby Burgess . . . formerly a cup-half-empty-man . . .
Starts believing in fairy tales
Starts believing in 'He lives happily ever after'
That
There might just be a cloud with a silver lining for him
There might be just a wee pot of gold at the end of this
particular rainbow . . .
Because
Slowly    but surely
In a world formerly full of *frogs* . . .
Some *princes* start tae emerge . . .
As
A lot of them
Just get *better*

(*And they do . . . as . . .*)


## FOURTEEN
### FOUR LIGHT YEARS LATER

*Boxers return to the gym . . .*
    *Older, fitter, better.*
    *They perform magnificently.*

**Bobby**
    I can see for myself    just a wee bit more money
    I can feel    the possibility of *success* . . .

Because I hit my lucky streak
Two nights turn to three into four into five
Things are starting to cook
The ingredients, the recipe's working
Talent's beginning to twinkle
Among the fighting frogs
I'm finding my princes . . . and . . .
Princes are like buses . . . you wait ages for one . . .
Then three or four come along all at once!

This is my hot prospect. (*Indicates Ajay.*)
Ajay 'The Cobra' Chopra

I'm pinning my hopes on this one
If I can just keep him *here*. (*Under his thumb.*)
Under *control*!

Born to it
Watch . . .
Speed     Intelligence . . . Talent

The one there . . .

'Professor' Ainsley Binnie

Steady hardworking but . . . no sure . . .
Too much . . . (*Taps his head.*) . . . too
'booksblogswebsitefact!' . . .

This one – (*Neil Neill.*)

Neil Neill
Fists of Steel
*Maniac* but on a good day *magic* . . .
You're just never sure when that day's gonnae *be* . . .

(*Dina next . . .*)

Look at this one, Dina Massie the Boxing Lassie . . .

(*She is brilliant.*)

If she were a lad . . .
I could take her to the top of the mountain
Make her the brightest star in the sky
We'd both have big huge houses
Our own Mercedes . . .

**Dina**
*BMWs.*

**Bobby**
If she'd only contemplate the world of *women's* boxing
She could . . .

**Dina**
Drive a Robin Reliant!

Live in a fucking *shed!*

If it's so wonderful put you're money where your
mouth is,
Bobby Burgess . . .

**Bobby**
Go away!

(*He pushes her away with the pads.*)

This one – (*Indicates Cameron.*)

Cameron Burns

great *instinctive* boxer brilliant stamina    joined me
late . . . still a bit behind still a bit
*attitude* . . . (*Performs attitude.*)
Nae Einstein . . .
Looks like a wee white mouse
But with the heart of a lion . . .
Seems like    a wee cheap ukulele
But plays like a Fender Stratocruiser . . .

Ajay Chopra!!!
I don't know what you're doing but you're no doing
what I told you!

**Ajay**
I'm trying something new.

**Bobby**
You're *trying* my patience!!!

**Ajay**
I just want you to consider something / I observed that might work . . .

**Bobby**
And *I* just want you to do as you're telled, you arrogant little bloody . . .!

(*Bobby moves away . . .*)

Nae bloody *showboating*!


### FIFTEEN
### THREE FAVOURITE SONS

**Bobby** (*to Dina*)
Show me your jab.

(*She does.*)

Rubbish

(*It isn't.*)

Show me your hook

(*She does.*)

Rubbish

(*It isn't.*)

I don't know why I bother

**Dina**
Yes you do.

**Dina/Bobby** (*separate worlds*)
'This is Sandy
He's your new stepdaddy
Say hello to Uncle Sandy.'
'Hello, Uncle Sandy.'
'Well you're a pretty wee girl come and sit on Uncle
Sandy's knee . . .'

**Bobby**
She's dafter than ever

**Dina**
Leopard

Spots

You should have married her.

**Bobby**
No, I should just have adopted *you*

You want *me* to come sort Uncle Sandy oot?

**Dina**
No. I'm a Big Girl.
I'll sort him oot *myself*.

**Bobby**
Boxing's no aboot *revenge*.

**Dina**
So wrong.
So old and   so wrong.

(*He touches her head.*
   *She punches him very lightly in the heart.*
   *They separate.*
   *Ainsley has seen this.*)

**Bobby**
Ainsley Binnie, what you looking at???

**Ainsley**
Nothing

**Bobby**
Look somewhere else

**Ainsley**
Okay

(*He looks away.*)

**Bobby**
And

Sort your hands out you, look like a fuckin boxing kangaroo!

(*Ainsley's hands go up.*)

Let's go let's go let's see you kill it

(*Watches Cameron.*)

Good
It's your shoulder carries your guard, Cameron Burns.
Watch *this maniac*.

(*Neil Neill punches. Cameron watches . . .*)

Just like I telled ye . . . *Good!*

Ajay Chopra
Cameron Burns
Neil Neill . . .

(*They all come up to him.*)

I want you to think about turning pro.

**Neil Neill**
*YESSSSS!!!*

**Cameron**
Fucking *ace!!!*

**Ajay**
I have already been thinking / this is a good plan

**Bobby**
I'm prepared to train you myself
Manage all your business and paperwork
But   it's *three* of you
It's a fuck of a lot of work from *me*
So I want two hundred per cent commitment from all
of *youse* . . .

**Cameron/Ajay/Neil**
Aye alright.

**Bobby**
I want you to talk to your parents

**Cameron**
Aye   *alright!!!!*

**Neil Neill**
Is it alright if it's my Care Coordinator, Bobby?

**Bobby**
Care Coordinator/Parents/Parole Officer whatever . . .

(*Ainsley has seen this.*)

Just a second . . .

Ainsley Binnie, what you looking at???

**Ainsley**
Nothing.

**Bobby**
Look somewhere else

**Ainsley**
Okay

(*He looks away . . .*)

**Bobby**

See if I can hook you up with a promoter, sort oot some money

**Ajay**

My uncle the property investor is interested in –

**Bobby**

Okay

**Ajay**

– discussing funding with you

**Bobby**

Early days yet . . . we want tae start slow and care / ful okay?

**Ajay**

He has a conglomerate of businessmen –

**Bobby**

Okay . . .

**Ajay**

– who
Have seed money –

**Bobby**

Early days . . .

**Ajay**

– that they're looking tae ring / fence –

**Bobby**

Read my lips. 'Early days.'

**Ajay**

– for a more / diversified project . . .

**Bobby**

*Early Days! Jeezus!!!*

(*They go back to work . . .*)

## SIXTEEN
## WHAT'S IN THE FRIDGE

*Carlotta has her head inside her fridge.*

**Carlotta**
I'm pretending I'm defrosting my fridge
I'm pretending I'm discovering what's hidden in the
frozen wastes of the freezer compartment . . .
It's snow white snow as far as the eye can see
and an iceberg the size of *Aberdeen*     he wants tae
turn professional!

Cool it!

Chillax!

(*She puts her head back into the cold.*)

(*From within the fridge.*) Noooooooooooooooooooooo!

(*She comes out of the fridge.*)

Just bear with me a moment . . .
Until I've processed this
Wrapped it in *cling film*
*Freezed* it and put it in here till its *Sell-By Date*
Like every other one of my *Terrors!!!*

*Amateur* . . .
He was *safe* . . .
*Professional* . . .
That's aboot people with the money saying
We've *paid* for this . . .
What we want is *blood*
What we want is *damage*
That's what we're paying tae see!

It'll be alright
It may never happen

Things come to nothing
Dreams die
Cool It!

(*And she puts her head back in the fridge.*)

### SEVENTEEN
### OUT INTO THE COLD COLD SNOW

*Bobby watching, sees Ajay humiliating his opponent . . .*

**Bobby**
Oh for *fuck's sake*!!!

*Showboating!*

*Again!!!*

*Again* with the *Humiliating*!

*What* did I tell you?

**Ajay**
You told me to do as you tell me

**Bobby**
So why didn't you *do* as I tell you?

Jesus *Christ*!!!

**Ajay**
Because   I don't always think you know better than me

**Bobby**
Don't you?

**Ajay**
Because   I have applied myself rigorously to the study
of my style
Which is significantly *different* from everybody else's
and . . .
Bloody *effective*.

**Bobby**

You think . . .???

**Ajay**

Yes.
And
And

Because    we should be able to discuss things . . . and
agree on strategies . . .
If I'm going pro we need to agree on a thought-through /
style of attack . . .

**Bobby**

Get your kit.

**Ajay**

What?

**Bobby**

Get your kit. And go.

(*He reaches in his pocket for some money.*)

Here . . . your subs back. Go spend it at another gym.
I need boxers who *know* who / knows best.

**Ajay**

I was just
Wait
No
This is banal. *BOBBY!!!*

**Bobby**

It's finished.
Over.

**Ajay**

I'm the best boxer here

(*Silence.*)

I have the best style.

(*Nothing.*)

The best brain.

(*Nothing.*)

I'm turning pro
You want me to turn pro.

(*Nothing.*)

You're my trainer . . .

(*Nothing.*)

*Bobby!*     This is *banal*. /
Can't we . . .

**Bobby**
   *Ajay!!!*
   Try *listen* for once!
   *Listening* is how you *learn*
   Hard Facts
   I'm gonnae be Cameron Burn's trainer.
   I'm gonna be Neil Neill's trainer
   I might even God help us be Ainsley Binnie's trainer

**Ainsley**
   *Yesss!*
   Thanks, Bobby!

**Bobby**
   No you.

**Dina**
   Thanks, Bobby

**Ajay**
   Can't we discuss this . . .?

   Are we not going to discuss this???

**Bobby**

*Discussing* is exactly what this is aboot!
I'm running a *boxing* gym, no *A Question ae Sport*!
Discipline's aboot *obedience*.

**Ajay**

Not *blind* obed / ience, shouldn't a boxer *think*???

**Bobby**

He should think aboot *boxing*
Nae *humiliation* of his opponent

**Ajay**

It helps tae *win*.

It's what the crowd *likes*.

(*Pause.*)

**Bobby**

Get your kit.
Get oot of my gym.
Find yourself somewhere that *likes* you tae win like that.

(*Beat. Will there be a real fight? Tears? A reverse decision . . .?*)

**Ajay**

Thank you, Bobby.

(*Kit.*)

I wish you every success.

(*Jacket on.*)

I wish everyone here every success.

(*Bag.*
  *Ajay leaves.*
  *Sticky silence.*)

**Bobby**
Ainsley Binnie

**Ainsley**
Bobby!

**Bobby**
Did you hear all that?

**Ainsley** (*lying*)
No, Bobby.

**Bobby**
Not absolutely definitely *you* yet, understand . . .?

**Ainsley**
Yes, Bobby.

**Bobby**
Ainsley Binnie!
Neil Neill!
Stairs!
Now!
Cameron Burns!
Dina Massie!
You two are finished now.

(*To Cameron.*) See the lassie safe home, okay?

**Cameron**
I'm no sure / the Lassie will *let* me see her safe home . . .

**Dina**
'The Lassie' can see herself / safe home!

**Bobby**
Just both o' you do what I bloody *tell* you!

(*Dina and Cameron leave together. Not pleased.*)

(*To us.*) You can't have a *democracy*
Your reign's got to be *absolute*!

(*To himself.*) Good Decision
Good decision!
*Fuck!!!*


## EIGHTEEN
### 'WE HAVE NOTHING BUT TIME'

*Cameron and Dina alone and exhausted somewhere . . .*

**Cameron**
What's the point?

**Dina**
What's what point?

**Cameron**
The point of *you*.

**Dina**
What?

**Cameron**
What's the point of *you* boxing?

**Dina**
What's the point of *you* boxing?

**Cameron**
I'm training tae a peak of superb physical fitness

**Dina**
I'm training tae a peak of superb physical fitness

**Cameron**
And . . .

**Dina**
And . . .?

**Cameron**
I'm going tae be a fuckin champion and fuckin famous
with a fistful of fuckin money

**Dina**

I'm going tae be fuckin toned and gorgeous and take nae shit frae any fuckin wannabee champion scrawny

*And* a fuckin champion

*And* fucking famous

With a fuckin *enormous* fistful o' fuckin money

*Beat.*

**Cameron**

Aye, whatever

(*Beat.*)

What's your name again?

**Dina**

You *know* what my fucking name is.

**Cameron**

Oh yes. Tits.

**Dina**

Tits o' *Terror*.

**Cameron**

Nice name.

O'Terror.

Is that Irish?

(*Not worth a response.*)

You want tae go for a drink?

**Dina**

Not till you've got yourself famous with your fistful of fuckin money.
'Fists'.

(*She leaves.*)

**Cameron** (*calls*)

It's a *date* then, 'Tits'?

(*Secretly.*) Dina

Cameron and Dina     *Burns*

(*Yes . . . it works . . .*)

Aye     alright

(*He hopes no one saw or heard this.*)


### NINETEEN
### NICE HANDS, YOUR PRECISION INSTRUMENTS

*Carlotta applying hand cream.*

**Carlotta**

It's okay
It's alright
It's all good.

Your honour
In mitigation of my crime in sending my only son
Intae the bloody mean money-grabbing manipulative
Face-mashing body-smashing world
Of professional boxing . . .
I would argue . . .

He's fucking *brilliant* at it!

It makes him *special* tae *the world*!

It shortens the odds on him *getting* somewhere in life.

There's an ootside chance my son's gonnae *count*!

(*She fastens up her hand cream. Regards her hands,
which are soft as snow.*)

These are *my* precision instruments
I'm gonnae be doing a lot o' clapping

Oh yes
A *lot* of clapping!

(*She exits.*)

## TWENTY
### THESE CRUELLY IGNORED BUT
### MOST RESILIENT OF THE BURGESS STABLE

*Ainsley Binnie somewhere, working hard.*
*Dina somewhere also, also working hard.*

**Ainsley**
Alright    Dina?

**Dina**
Can't see you

**Ainsley**
If you need any help back-up feedback / type thing

**Dina**
Can't hear you

**Ainsley**
Occupied. Right?
Focused. Right?
I get it.
Respect.

(*Ainsley goes away . . . but . . .*)

**Bobby**
Ainsley Binnie.

**Ainsley**
Yes, Bobby?

**Bobby**
Okay.
Thing is . . .

I'm a bit *pressed* with Cameron and Neil and their
schedules and setting up matches and paperwork and
legwork and shite . . .

**Ainsley**
Yes, Bobby.

**Bobby**
I have tae *prioritise*
So I'm *devolving* you tae Auld Alec and Whammo for
training.

**Ainsley**
Oh. But . . . Couldn't . . . It's just . . .
Auld Alec and Whammo . . .?

**Bobby**
They'll be able tae give you more time than I can . . .

**Ainsley**
But . . .

Okay Yes Bobby. Got it
Understand /
Completely.

**Bobby**
Good lad.

(*He exits.*
    *Ainsley sits down somewhere. Body blow. The*
*heart.*
    *Dina on punchbags. She works furiously.*
    *Neil Neill enters. Takes over her bag.*)

**Dina**
What the fuck?

**Neil Neill**
Precedence thing.
Pro stuff.
Bobby says.

(*Dina moves to the next punchbag.*
*Both work them.*
*Cameron enters.*)

**Cameron**  (*to Dina*)
Alright?

**Dina**
Alright.

**Cameron**
Bobby says I have tae put three minutes in on this . . .
Pro stuff
Preference thing

(*Her punchbag.*
*He waits.*)

**Dina**
Shit.
Okay.

(*She makes way for him.*
*He punches furiously.*)
*She watches.*)

Good.

**Cameron**
I've got tae concentrate
No distractions.
Bobby says.

(*Dina goes to a space. Shadow punches.*)

**Ainsley**
This cruelly ignored but still unbeaten supermiddleweight
This most resilient of the Burgess stable
Learns the hardest lesson of his career . . .
Patience     that virtue of the very best
He needs to get *Zen*

He's quite spiritual, this imperious quietly impressive
contender . . .
Pushed to the limits of his considerable ability
Regarded as the underdog
His time will come . . .

(*He watches Dina.*)

No . . . Dina

(*He gets up . . .*)

Sweetheart    You need to . . .

(*He gets hold of her to show her a technique . . . but it
is the final straw . . .*)

**Dina**
Jesus fuckin Christ just some space just some fuckin
*space*!!!

(*And she turns and lashes out at him.*
    *It surprises him.*
    *It fells him.*)

Not all!
Not half!
Just some!!!

**Ainsley**
I don't know what you're talking / aboot . . .
I was just trying to help

**Dina**
No! You don't!
Fact!

**Ainsley**
That was just    lucky.

**Dina**
That was *boxing*!

D'you   even *know* how good I am???
D'you even know how much I like to fuckin *love*
The sweat the hittin the punching the –
How much I want tae hit be hit compete get blooded
up feel someone's nose bones go crunch under my
hand
Feel the fuckin breath leave somebody's fuckin
stomach???
Punch me back!

**Ainsley**

No.

**Dina**

Punch me back, you fuckin coward.

**Ainsley**

No.

**Dina**

So you punch me in the breast?
So you put me on the floor?
I'll *kill* you!!!
Fuckin punch me!!!!

**Ainsley**

I don't *want* to!!!

(*He doesn't know what he's done but . . .*)

Sorry, Dina.

**Dina**

Oh   *fuck!!*

(*She realises where she is heading . . .*)

No

*I'm* sorry

Boxing's about skill and discipline.

(*She collects her stuff . . .*)

No about *rage*.

It's too dangerous.

I shouldnae be here.

I'm not a boxer
I'm a *killer*

(*Exiting . . . She comes back.*)

And . . .

Ainsley . . .

It *was* just lucky.

Sorry.

(*And she's out. She passes . . . some way from the ring.*)


### TWENTY-ONE
### TWO AJAYS

*Ajay in very expensive warm-up gear.*

**Ajay**
Every day's mad . . . be the figurehead on this project
Be the Name on that project . . .
I glaze over.
It's like there's two Me's.
I'm not just Ajay Chopra.
I'm Ajay Chopra, pro boxer     Contender.
Role model. Icon.
Asian Star.
The Spitting Cobra!

One God, Bobby???
One King?

69

Don't think so.

Time
Is eternal and cyclical
The closing of one door
Implies the opening of another.

I am full of *joy*

I am full of celebration

That's why I'm always happy and calm

That's why I am hard to *read*.

(*He feints in a Prince Naseem-type way. He punches.*)

And surprising,
Short Punjabi History lesson Bobby Bloody Burgess!

My rhythms are hundreds of years old
my roots are long and strong and deep
Into the ground . . .
This is why it is so hard to knock me off my feet
I am *rooted*
The ground is *mine*
It's what makes me a *Winner*
It's what makes me *Win*
*This* is the champion!   Here!   *This!*
Fuck you, Bobby Burgess . . .

(*He circles . . .*)

Watch what happens, *Bobby Burgess.*

Let me hit you, let the champion hit you.

(*The combination of punches from the final round,
fells an invisible opponent . . .*)

Don't get up
Don't.

Joy for me boy, joy.

## TWENTY-TWO
## BREATH

*Neil Neill and Cameron, utterly out of breath, trying to catch any air whatever. Until . . .*

**Neil Neill**
*Fucking Bobby!*

**Cameron**
That *bastard!*

**Neil Neill**
He's *killing* us!

**Cameron**
*Right.*

The *bastard.*

D'you watch Ajay last night?

**Neil Neill**
Bloody *brilliant*!

*Magic!*

**Cameron**
Could *you* take him?

**Neil Neill**
Could I???

Put Me in a Ring with Him, Bobby Fucking Burgess!

Could You???

**Cameron**
Could I???

Get Me the Fucking Contest, Bobby!!!
I'll knock his fucking head off his fucking shoulders

I'll punch his fucking lights out
I'll put him doon
He'll never get up
If you'd just pull your fucking finger out
And promote the fuck oot of me
And put me up against him
Bobby fucking Burgess . . .

(*Bobby walks in.*)

**Both** (*utmost cheeriness and politeness*)
Hey, Bobby!

Alright, Bobby!

(*And they're ready for . . .*)


### TWENTY-THREE
### ARRESTED PUNCHES

*Bobby is putting the gloves on Cameron and Neil.*

**Bobby**
Where we're at at this particular moment in time is
as follows . . . I'm talking tae Frank Warren Frank
Warren's talking tae Chopra's fuckin uncles and
*Entourage* and shite so we basically got a shot at the
Asian Super-Cobra once we're all agreed on the nuts
and fucking bolts . . .
But only *one* o' you shites can be *first* . . .
The decision is *mine*
It's all still tae play for
Okay
Contestants
The Time has come

Let's see you think for yourselves

(*Timer goes . . .*

*Neil and Cameron really go for each other . . .*
*A mini-bout . . . a minute.*
*Real time, then . . .*
*Slow time.*
*Within which they examine various of their punches.*

*Neil Neill punches Cameron's face. He examines the locking out of his arm.*

*Cameron puts a punch into Neil Neill's side.*

*Neil Neill puts a punch into Cameron's stomach . . .)*

**Cameron**
Look, Bobby
*Your* brain is in *ma* head
*Your* expertise is in *ma* hands
Your dreams are in *here.* (*His heart.*)

(*Cameron puts a right to Neil Neill's chin.*

*Neil Neill puts a blow to Cameron's jaw.*)

**Neil Neill**
Twenty-seven bones
to *one* bone
Get me Ajay, Bobby.

**Cameron**
Let me get Ajay.

(*They are equally matched.*
  *Timer buzzer goes.*)

**Bobby** (*to Neil Neill*)
Good that, Neil Neill.

(*To Cameron.*) Good that, Burns Boy . . .

(*To both.*) Showers!

(*Cameron and Neil grin at each other. Touch gloves.*)

**Cameron**
*Friends* . . .

Ya bastard

**Neil Neill**
*Ditto* . . .

Ya bastard . . .

(*They take out their water bottles.*
  *Lose . . . next.*)

You want tae come round my house?
I've got the *Rocky* box set!
*Rocky 1, 2, 3, 4* and *5*!
You want tae come watch *Rocky?*
Aye of course you do!!!

**Cameron**
Sure        in a bit.

(*Neil does the famous Rocky run, arms up . . .*)

**Neil Neill** (*fairly good Stallone impersonation*)
 I'm the Italian stallion . . .

I'm the Best!

**Cameron** (*his ripped vest*)
Oh *fuck*!
Look at this *vest*!

(*It's ripped.*)

Sixty-five fucking *quid*!
Cameron's making shite money

(*To anybody.*) Cameron's nae social life
Cameron's scrabbling around for a match
But
Cameron's a *pro* boxer
He's Somebody Tae *Watch*!!!

But . . .
*And* where's he gonna get the suede lockdoon hi-top
boots at £135, pro-fight gloves at £150 the pair new
punch mitts focus mitts handwraps bag gloves he
needs he's fucking haemorrhaging money . . .???

Fuck!

(*To the world.*) Let me have it!

It's not much to ask!
Then
I start tae earn
No more scratching around for coins
Subbing off your parents!
Soon you're saying . . .
'Here Mum, treat yourself,'
'Dad . . . buy yourself a *car*      the *Audi Megane* . . .?
No problem!
Mum?    D'you like this house?
Here. Keys!
Whose?
Mine! I bought it with my advertising???
For you.
It's yours.
Who do I run into?
Hey, Tits!
Hey      Dina
Yes . . .
That *was* me on the telly yes . . .
Yes . . . noo . . . with lassies . . . It *is* like Bees round
this Honeypot oh yes . . .
I warned you tae
Date early tae avoid disappointment!

(*And he's gone . . .*)

## TWENTY-FOUR
## BOXING IS SAFER THAN CROSSING A ROAD

*Ainsley is in the dark deserted gym . . . talking to a non-existent Dina . . .*

**Ainsley** (*in answer to an admiring Dina's question*)
Yes!

Since I sought out alternative medicine
touch wood never been ill.
My immune system is immaculate.
Fact.

Two litres of water and 100 mg of Vitamin C every four hours
Vit C is a natural virus fighter so fresh OJ or a peeled orange . . . magic

I don't think . . . if you tried *now* . . . you'd be able to land one on me again!

That was funny wasn't it!
That was hilarious!

So Dina . . .

You want to hear something else funny?
Something really hilarious . . .?

(*A tiny sound somewhere in the darkness . . .*)

Okay . . .
If you play by *the rules* . . .
Boxing . . .

(*Another sound.*)

It's statistically safer than crossing a road!

(*Suddenly the dark is full of danger . . .*
    *Dimly, we can see someone in the shadows.*)

It's all about *supervision* . . .
*Structure* . . .
*Safety*     that's why they –

(*Neil Neill, with a can of Special Brew starts to prowl.*)

– check you immediately before the fight

(*Ainsley tries to keep him in range.*)

Eyes Mouth Ears Back It's a Game It's a Sport
It's mostly about

(*Neil Neill drinks some Special Brew . . .*)

Surprise
Surprise
Not power!

(*Neil Neill drinks . . .*)

Lungs Heart

(*And drinks . . .*)

The game's simple . . .
administer a shock to the nervous system

(*And drinks . . .*)

Overload his brain . . .
So it crashes
Hands Forearms Nintendo but with a real body
Right?

(*Neil Neill is getting nearer . . .*)

The last death in amateur boxing here in Scotland
Was *1952*!
Fact.

Accidents in boxing even professional boxing
Are rarer than you might / think and
Okay   the BMA *are* totally against boxing

But    honestly . . .
The studies are inconclusive . . .
Boxing isn't even the most dangerous / sport!
Fact!

(*He's now very close.*)

**Neil Neill**
Good tae know!

**Ainsley**
Try horseriding!

**Neil Neill**
Giddee *up*!

**Ainsley**
They keep five beds at the hospital
Every Saturday night
For *Rugby*
Fact.

**Neil Neill**
Up and under!

**Ainsley**
Climbing Ben Nevis is more danger / ous

**Neil Neill**
Don't say

**Ainsley**
Mostly    injury-wise    you're lucky

Fact.

(*Neil Neill* has *to attack Ainsley* . . .)

**Neil Neill**
Okay . . .
Here's a *Fact* . . .
Boxing never hurts *me* . . .

*I'm* no a statistic o' boxing
I'm crossing Renfield Street one Saturday night oot . . .
Fucking *taxi* full of lassies on a *hen* night I don't see it
comin
Bosh!!!
'Are ye alright, pal . . .
give us yer hand . . .
och what's happened tae yer hand???'

(*Film of the delicate bones of the hand all broken . . .*)

'And look at his leg his leg his leg's oh *cripes* . . .'

(*Film of the bones of the leg . . .*)

I'm a statistic o' drink / driving!

*Life* fucks me
No boxing.
Nae bother . . . plenty of boxers about . . .
Let's stick Cameron 'Fists of Fury' Burns in against
Ajay Chopra the Fighting Fuckin Cobra in instead o'
you
Turns me intae a *spectator*
*Total fucking spectator!!!*

(*A crowd of boozed-up Neil Neills appear behind him.*)

Oooo look . . .

(*From his civvies somewhere he produces . . .*)

A ringside seat ticket tae the championship contest
between Ajay Chopra and late substitution Cameron
'Fists ae Fury' Burns!!!

Now    *that's* funny!!!!

That's *hilarious*!

(*He drinks. He spectates . . .*)

## TWENTY-FIVE
## TWELVE THREE–MINUTE ROUNDS

*TV Screen monitors:* FRANK WARREN FRIDAY FIGHT NIGHT.

*Both are sitting quietly in their dressing rooms, waiting, as Bobby prepares Cameron . . .*
*Then:*

**Bobby**
Good luck      son

**Cameron**
Thank you      Mr Burgess.

**Bobby**
Ready?

**Cameron**
Aye   alright

(*Then . . . the most beautiful, sparse, complex dance of a twelve-round boxing match. It goes like this:*

*Steve George, the referee, is joined by two other dancing referees. A synchronised trio, they perform a dance of referees, semaphores, signals, tics and signifiers.*

*One strips off. She becomes:*
*Dina, in her too-high heels, too-tight shorts, too revealing top. She looks as physically bound as an ancient footbound Chinese courtesan.*

*She struts round the ring, and does the look-at-my-crotch stance at each side.*)

**Dina** (*to us*)
You can wipe that 'what the fuck's she daeing there?' off your faces.

You'll all watch me for twelve rounds now, won't
you???

(*To baying crowd, smiling, posing seductively the
while:*)

I'm wind I'm sleet I'm storm I'm black clouds
I'm 'Get 'em oot fe the lads' . . . I'm 'Camel Toe!'
I'm 'A'd Gie Her One!' I'm the worst weather front
you'll ever meet!
Don't fuckin come near me . . .
Don't fuckinthinkabootit!
I'll pull your balls off and stuff them doon your
gawpingaspinthroat so you can have them for
breakfast!!!
I'll kill you!

(*To us.*) Different ways of being a 'Killer', right
This is what training and discipline does for you . . .
Plus a little bit of judicious silicon . . .

(*Then . . .*)
   *Steve George enters. Referee movement.*
   *Cameron and Ajay enter. To their corners.*
   *Steve George calls them to the centre and talks to
them.*
   *Boxers to their corners. They shake out.*
   *Bell. They box.*
   *As they box, Dina weaves between them, holding
high a round-card saying* ROUND ONE.
   *They fight.*
   *Bell. Cameron is in his corner. Bobby and Ainsley,
his seconds, move him about on his stool with towels
and send him, too early, back into the fight, where
Ajay has been circling him the while, shadow-
punching. Seconds away.*
   *They box.*
   *Dina weaves another seductive path through the
fighting with a card:* ROUND FOUR.

*In the fight, Ajay becomes temporarily deaf. The
music is muffled, odd.*

*Carlotta, stiff drink in hand, swaps her numbing
opiate with Dina for her round-card. Carlotta
completes the female interweaving of stance and card:*
ROUND SEVEN. *Cameron is stunned by a punch. The
inner revolve travels him, as the back wall projects
inside his head. Things are breaking in there.*

*He begins to regain his focus. He warms up and . . .*
*Gets smashed into* ROUND TEN.

*Dina performs a Spearmint Rhino solo in which she
is boxed about by an invisible opponent, while still
strutting and posing.*

*Steve George performs solo referee movements.*
ROUND TWELVE *card.*

*The boxers, tired, still fight fiercely.*

*Last bell. Cameron collapses, Steve George disappears.
Ajay, his arms raised in victory, disappears.*

### TWENTY-SIX
### BEAUTIFUL BURNOUT!

*Cameron is alone in the ring.*
*He receives the blows which have been punching him.*
*Three refs dress him . . .*

**Cameron**

Stars

Oh    *look!*

(*He can suddenly see . . .*)

Stars

I was *going* somewhere . . .?

(*Where was he going?*)

Fuuuuuuuuuuuuuuuuuuuuuuuuuuck    Stars!

Red planet Mars
Ma's
Look Ma, top of the world

*(He is still being hit but . . . he sees only . . .*
*Film of beautiful night sky with stars and planets . . .)*

Jupiter
Earth
Uranus *(That's very funny.)* ha ha
Saturn Mars bars *(That's odd.)*
Jupiter
Earth
Earth
Earth
Earth

*(Something breaks in his brain.)*
. . .
. . .
. . .
. . .
. . . what the . . .?

*(He sees something he has never seen before from*
*somewhere he has never been.)*
. . .
Oh fu—
oh well . . .

*(But he still sees only . . .)*

Joooo
Yur
Saaaaa
Mmmm      mmmmm
Ur
Ur
Ur

*(The light from these stars goes out too.*
*He cannot see anything.)*


## TWENTY-SEVEN
## REFEREE DANCE

*Steve George, in the ring but with remote, looks at*
*footage of one particular moment from the fight.*
*Dina, Bobby, Ainsley, in street clothes, dress him.*

**Steve George**
Watch like an eagle

Protect the boxer
Without fear or favour

'Referee Steve George's questionable refereeing in the
twelfth round'
Fuckin YouTube!!!
100,000 hits
Gotta *love* modern technology.

Let's see that *again*, Boxing Aficionados . . .

*(And presses replay.*
*Screen . . .*

*And presses replay.*
*And . . .)*


## TWENTY-EIGHT
## ONE PUNCH CAN GO ROUND THE WORLD
## FACT

*All over the space the other characters going about their*
*everyday lives.*
*But the punch that destroyed Cameron's brain travels*
*through their bodies with increasing intensity . . .*

**Ainsley**

There's this term, 'Black Lights'
In the Science World . . .
It's the black portion of the electromagnetic spectrum
Which is the domain of X-rays and radio waves.

**Bobby**

Okay
Ah might have made a wrong call    a few wrong calls
Maybe I should have thrown in the towel

(*He's putting up punchbags, equipment . . .*)

But
I didnae
Hey
Even *God* makes mistakes

**Ainsley**

It's also a term in boxing . . .
Some boxers report seeing 'black lights'
Just before oblivion
They *see* and become *surrounded* by
This shimmering    glowing aura of darkness

**Bobby**

I visit Cameron
Once a month
On a Sunday
That's my only day off

**Ainsley**

This shimmering darkness
Is known medically as 'visual scotoma'
The afflicted brain is experiencing the paradox
Of being *conscious* of its *unconsciousness.*

**Dina**

Well
He got what he wanted
He got tae fight with the whole world watching

He went twelve rounds
He defended himself tae the last
And
He *is* famous in a way.

**Ajay**
I won
I'm unconquerable
I remember *everything*.

Breathe in

(*He breathes in.*)

Breathe out

(*He falters . . .*)

**Bobby**
Don't believe in fairy tales
You have tae move on
You get one life
Time doesnae stand still
I make a call
I take over the training o' this likely lad frae Greenock.
His brains are in his hands
He doesnae try tae hurt the air
And
He's *lucky*.

**Ainsley**
The *reason* for this black lights phenomenon
When the higher cognitive centres of the brain shut
down
The lower areas
The *limbic* system
Kick in to preserve a primitive sense of awareness
Our human system sort of *organises* itself to *defend*
itself . . .

It's brilliant

It's *made* to fight
It *loves* fighting,    the human body

Fact.

**Neil Neill**
What spectators do
Is
*Watch*
I take my *Rocky* box round tae Cameron
We watch it all the time
That
And
*The Champ*
Except
*The Champ*'s a bit *sad* for us . . .
We both greet like wee lassies . . .


TWENTY-NINE
BLACK LIGHTS

*Carlotta brings on a bag of laundry.*
    *A washing line appears.*
    *She starts pegging out washing, from baby clothes to*
*fully grown man . . .*
    *She tries as always for cheeriness, humour and the*
*bright side . . .*
    *Carlotta's doing laundry.*

**Carlotta**
Good news is

(*It takes a while but she tries to mean this . . .*)

I get my little boy back
I get my baby

My Cameron
I get him every minute of every hour of every day of
every week
Of every year but I get him back . . .

(*Carlotta goes to Cameron. This is secret.*)

My stripy wee cat.

You're supposed to see stars
I hope you do
I hope you don't just see dark
I hope you see sky
Blue sky      sun
Or
The night sky
Wi shooting stars

What you got in your head, darlin?

What can you see, son?

(*Inside Cameron's head is a boxing gym.*
*He is sparring.*
*He is boxing.*
*Everyone is sparring and boxing and fighting for life.*
*He smiles.*)

*End of Play.*